How Can I Look It Up When I Don't Know How It's Spelled?

Spelling Mnemonics and Grammar Tricks

How Can I Look It Up
When I Don't Know How It's Spelled?

Spelling Mnemonics and Grammar Tricks

by

Marjorie Maddox

© 2024 Marjorie Maddox. All rights reserved.
This material may not be reproduced in any form, published,
reprinted, recorded, performed, broadcast,
rewritten or redistributed without
the explicit permission of Marjorie Maddox.
All such actions are strictly prohibited by law.

Cover design by Shay Culligan
Cover image by busracavus/iStock
Author photo by Melanie Rae Buonavolonta

ISBN: 978-1-63980-540-2

Kelsay Books
502 South 1040 East, A-119
American Fork, Utah 84003
Kelsaybooks.com

Acknowledgments

Thank you to the following publications, in which versions of these poems previously appeared:

Ethel: "The Resi**stance** Took Its Stance"

Poetry Motel: "There's Iron in This Env**iron**ment"

The Short of It (She Writes It Press)*:* "A Double Helping of *S*, Please," "Double the Consonants, Shorten the Vowel," "I Take My Coff**ee** with Two *E*s," "There Is a Rat in the Middle of Sep**arat**e"

This book includes images selected and compiled by Karen Elias using licensed Clip Art, as well as several of her original drawings, for which I am extremely grateful.

*To my students of all ages
and to the teachers everywhere
who make learning fun*
—MM

Contents

How Can I Look It Up When I Don't Know How It's Spelled?	13
When Two Vowels Go Walking,	15
Double the Consonant, Shorten the Vowel	17
Roar Vowels	19
I Before *E* Except After *C*	21
There Is a Rat in the Middle of Sep**arat**e	23
There's Iron in This Env**iron**ment	25
There's an Ant on the Defend**ant**	27
The Resi**stance** Took Its Stance	29
"The LL in Para**ll**el Gives Me 'El,"	31
I Take My Cof**fee** with Two *E*s	33
A Double Helping of *S,* Please	35
Loose as a Goose	37
Loose Loses an *O*	39
There Is a Double Ass in **Assass**in	41
The Princi**pal** Is Your Pal	43
Its/It's	45
I/Me	47
Whoever, Whomever—Whatever!	49
Diagramming Directions	51

Preface

Welcome to this book for the grammar-obsessed and the spelling-challenged, for those who adore the rules of language and those who flee in terror. *How Can I Look It Up When I Don't Know How It's Spelled?* is here to help with mnemonics, that magician's memory bag of tricks. Here are poetic riffs on the familiar, the humorous, and the sometimes unexpected sayings that guide English spelling—"*I* Before *E* Except After *C*," "There Is a Rat in the Middle of Se**parat**e," "There Is a Double Ass in **Assass**in"—as well as such grammatical guidelines as when to use *I* or *me*, *whoever* or *whomever*, *it's* or *its*.

Watch what happens when two vowels go walking, when a loose goose breakdances in Brooklyn, and when the resi**stance** takes a stance. Coupled with lively illustrations, these witty reflections on orthography and basic language principles encourage newcomers and experts alike to consider when to devour dessert in the desert or how to determine if, truly, "the princi**pal** is your pal." Read, enjoy, share, remember!

How Can I Look It Up
When I Don't Know How It's Spelled?

Start with the sound the noun makes
when it's stubborn, when it won't soar
from your tongue. Pa-
lane putt-putting on Tastebud Runway.
Move to the *L* and listen
as it curls back in its flip, then plunges,
a nose-dive toward teeth, past
any air threatening gingivitis.
Aim at the *A* and hold
that thought steady with the horizon.
Now bite down on the *N,* nip it
in the right gear, don't pull up,
steady, steady, steady, smooth, now
de-accelerate, on with the brakes,
aviate that word smack
in its lane: page 1002, column one.

When Two Vowels Go Walking,

the first chatters, jabbers, prattles,
cackles, gibbers, babbles,
mutters, sputters, splutters,
rattles, clatters, blathers all the way past Baker Street,
around the ballfield and back. It is usually the *O,*
her whole body a wind tunnel of what, who, why, where, and when
her neighbors are doing, thinking, saying.
It is easy to get caught in the whirl
as her arms aerobically push away with their weights
any oncoming interruption.
Best to take an iPhone and not listen.

The second, the *A,* too shy for assertiveness training,
left out of Friends and Family,
is resigned to the single scene. She simply walks.
Nodding acknowledgment at each step,
she is at home as audience,
her aphonia altogether alluring
to those mouthing the monologue.

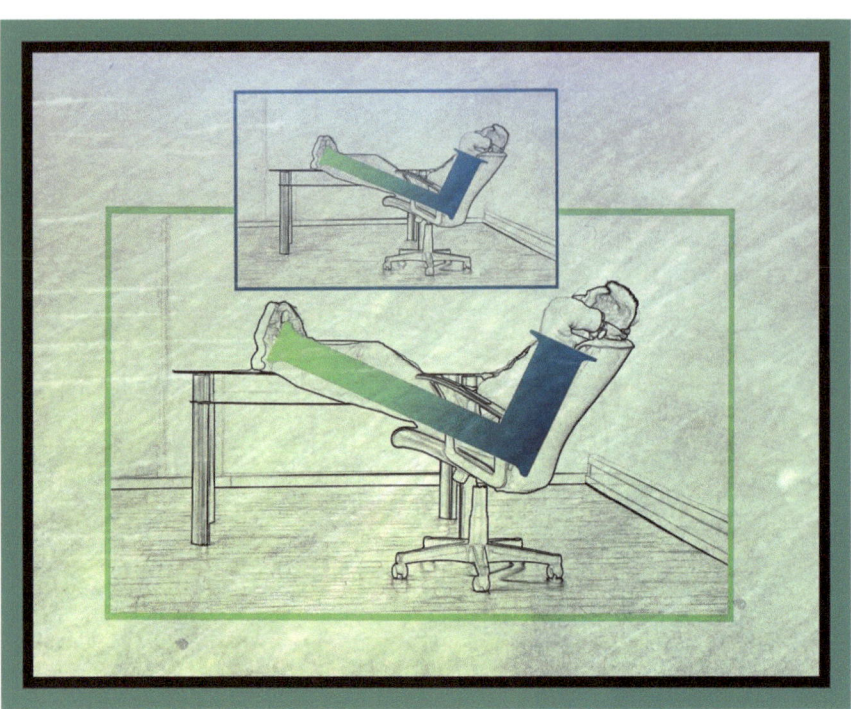

Double the Consonant, Shorten the Vowel

That's what comes from majority rule:
the *T*s stretching their crossbeams further
across better, *G*s claiming they're bigger,
*L*s lazily lounging with their political pull,
*P*s too dippy with twin happiness to notice
their former association with pain and poverty.

O *O*s and silent *A*'s,
diminutive *i*'s, *E*s eager to please and acquiesce,
and, of course, the once ubiquitous *U*,
whoop, roar, hoot, scream, screech
above the clamor of consonants
already claiming house control of *hubbub,
commotion, applause.*

Roar Vowels

It starts as a yawn turned *O*,
opens to more,
a groan stretching between teeth,
then an exhilarating *EEEEEEE* screech
when vowels pounce
and the cave-mouth echoes horror
before a solitary *I*.

Hungry is the *U-*
phemism that sweeps blood
beneath the purr
that comes after
when paws are clean,
the tongue licking
the leftover *A*.

I Before *E* Except After *C*

Ever a Clark Kent gentleman,
e steps aside for politeness,
letting his fr**ie**nd go first:
*bel**ie**ve, retr**ie**ve, ach**ie**ve.*

Behold the open mouth of *C,*
scary and carnivorous,
a conspicuous coward-turned-bully,
crunching his crooked bicuspids at *i,*
who is, after all, just a little thing,
tiny and timid, shivering with fright
on the sidelines.

Unable to shake h**ei**ght and w**ei**ght,
e concedes modestly, leads out of necessity.
No surprise: *e*'s a hero in disguise,
speedy to rec**ei**ve the brunt of *C*'s scowl,
willing to sh**ie**ld his fr**ie**nd
from *misconc**ei**ve* and *dec**ei**ve.*

The rat's tail snaps out like nun-chucks,
reels in the red meat of the rational,
the tough but tenuous topic sentences
        tied together
just-so with brown paper and transitions,

sepa  e

but no address,
"Undeliverable" stamped across the letters
before they're tossed.

There Is a Rat in the Middle of Sep**arat**e

not just his teeth, as pointed as before-test pencils,
but his entire seamy body gleams
with longing for the lost
spelling bee, its airborne script
intercepted by the evolved, phonically
abused, and chomping pterodactyl,
who took the tiny sting like a man
sucking on sore taste buds
and flew off to a museum to sulk.

The rat's tail snaps out like nun-chucks,
reels in the red meat of the rational,
the tough but tenuous topic sentences tied together
just-so with brown paper and transitions,
but no address,
"Undeliverable" stamped across the letters
before they're tossed.

In this garbage can of sound and lost vowels,
there must be, the rat sneers,
bones worth chewing, homonyms half-digested,
picked over and passed on
by Spelling Checkers. And he digs deeper
into the pile of mismatched prefixes,
misspelled *bannanna peals*; he digs deeper
into the tunnels of proclaimed typos; he digs deeper
sniffing, sniffing, sniffing,
day-dreaming always of Limburger
accurately spelled.

what happened
to green pastures, still waters?

env  ment

Restore them. O Lord,
let us lie down once again
beside letters.

There's Iron in This Env**iron**ment

but what's it worth to unearth
the word, soil the soil with steamrollers,
steam shovelers, sour-faced men sweating
illiterately in the sun? What happened
to green pastures, still waters?
Restore them. O Lord,
let us lie down once again
beside letters. Let us choose
the holier-than-thou path of proofreaders.
Let us resist the evil industrialist
mass-producing mechanical error.
Yea, for the environment is surely the author's
and the glory thereof.

There's an Ant on the Defend**ant**

surreptitiously
circling the ear.
Will he spill

into the
auricle when the
gavel galvanizes the guilty
for, once again, guessing
the wrong ending? Will his
abdomen, stitched together
like red ellipses, twirl
about the tympanum,
a whirlpool waiting
to happen?

He took a wrong
turn on his way to a
picnic and ended up (so pitiful!)
on the prosecutor's list. The jury is all
editors, the judge a perfectionist. Where
are the others in his army? Independently,
this star witness is a wimp and won't withstand
cross-examination. His only chance is to chant
his *genus* to a man now chewing hyphens
across pencils. Do the errors require
incarceration? The ant's not after
retaliation, just remorse, a simple
admission of guilt, recognition
of injustice served daily
to the misspelled,
the uncorrected.

The Resi**stance** Took Its Stance

and refused to support any sentence
until recognized for the phoneme it is. The defiance
of detail had gone on long enough.
"I, too, am a word," it shouted and,
sticking an exclamation in a wayward footnote,
rallied all subordinate territory. Activist,
union leader, *A. N. C. E.* charter member
(against non-cooperative elitists), Resistance
knew the jots and tittles of strike,
organized until midnight,
passed out placards, took its people
right to the steps of the title, then demanded
(non-violently) an audience with the author.

"The LL in Parallel Gives Me 'El,"

Mr. Vanshuskin—homeroom teacher,
Cub Scout master, would-be
mathematician and literary critic
of the second, third, and fourth grades—
explained systematically (straightening that crooked tie)
each time he tap-tapped his chalk
in somewhat parallel lines, generously scouting boundaries
across his slate expanse of wilderness
for our wobbly print or script.

We passed spelling by failing
penmanship. (What he couldn't read
couldn't be deducted,
subtracted, or in any way taken from
our rags-to-rags George Washington
Grammar School average.) Still,
everyone's vocabulary escalated
on the playground, where we dropped
our *h*s daringly behind backs,
chanting in unison beneath breaths, "to 'el
with the double *L* in parallel"
all the way round the four-square
courts and defiantly into adulthood.

I Take My Coff**ee** with Two *E*s

two *F*s and no artificial sweetener;
my sherbet, please (so low-fat), with an extra *r*,
my filet mignon with its *g* and *n*
tenderly underdone.

Ah vichyssoise à la Ritz,
bouillabaisse, asparagus vinaigrette,
salmon dipped and smoked.
Ah, Grand Marnier soufflés,
peppermint-chocolate mousse—why wait

for the weight of words
to ingest each letter
by letter? Such sweet
seasoning to the palate,
basted sound and roasted syllable.
Ah, Messieurs et Mesdames,
the delicacy, the delight,
the culinary delectableness of language
skillfully marinated, prepared,
and presented by that master
Webster.

A Double Helping of *S,* Please

Yes, I'll take another *s* in my de**ss**ert,
another slice of strudel,
an extra sampling of strawberry shortcake,
a smidgen more of spritz, twin pecan tassies,
double cheesecake snack squares.

No thank you, please, not a single de**s**ert,
that dusty Sahara sandbox
where I crave scores of sibilations
to satisfy this persistent thirst
for all that's sweet and sugary.

Loose as a Goose

breakdancing on the broken sidewalks of Brooklyn,
between beats gargling bad air,
breathing oxygen, deep, deep, deep
till it tingles the ends of its psychedelically
webbed feet, its bill a billion lyrics spinning
out across the airways. Even so,
in its almost dead-as-a-duck euphoria,
it can sing, it can dance, it can spell
inhale and *potato*.

Loose Loses an *O*

and can't find it anywhere.
It was her great-great
grandmother's and worth
a letter. I have it
beneath my mattress, flat as
a note that has nowhere
to go but the local dead letter
office, where it's not worth
the stamp to read too late how your great-
great grandmother lost it,
psychologically speaking, and has
willed all her letters to charity. Great
gods, she lived nowhere
on this planet. And as
for me and my new acquisition, it
can't hurt to be worth
a letter more, not less, as
I, past and undeniably worthy
winner of those great
word games, where
everyone not me loses
it, psychologically speaking. As
far as I know, nowhere
else on the board is a word worth
what I'm thinking now. It's
great to be alive, and as
the owner of an *O* and the where-
withal to score great
numbers with worthy
syllables such as
these: *Quotidian*. Great
gods, what a sound!

There Is a Double Ass in **Assass**in

A Push-Me-Pull-You folded;
a mule mass-produced, married;
a burro bundled with another:
all piled high with *what*s and *which not*s
of whom to catch and how soon
by every correctly spelled spy
in closed-captioned movies.

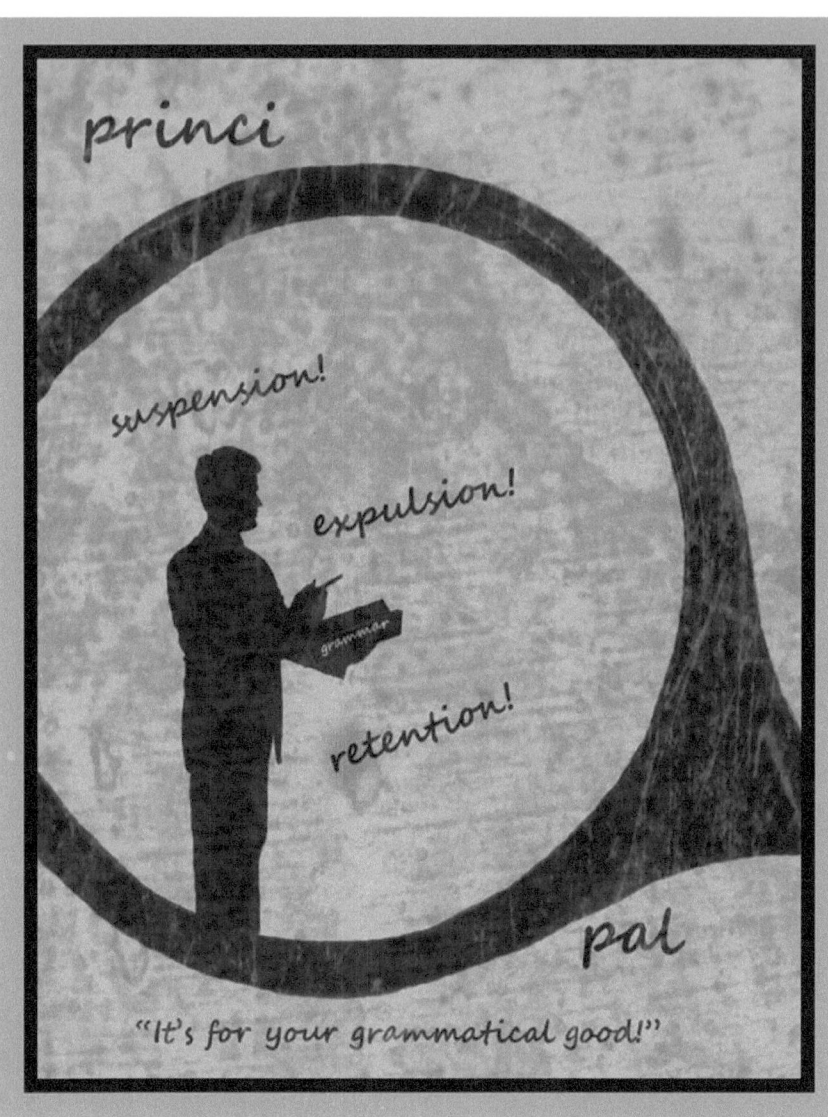

The Princi**pal** Is Your Pal

supposedly, but with what principles, boasting so
prince-like from his authoritarian office
of spelling rights and wrongs? The final word
on retention, suspension, expulsion,
he compulsively claims to edit, credit, and correct
for our grammatical good, this Lord of Letters
deceptively citing friendship
as sentence-rule addendum.

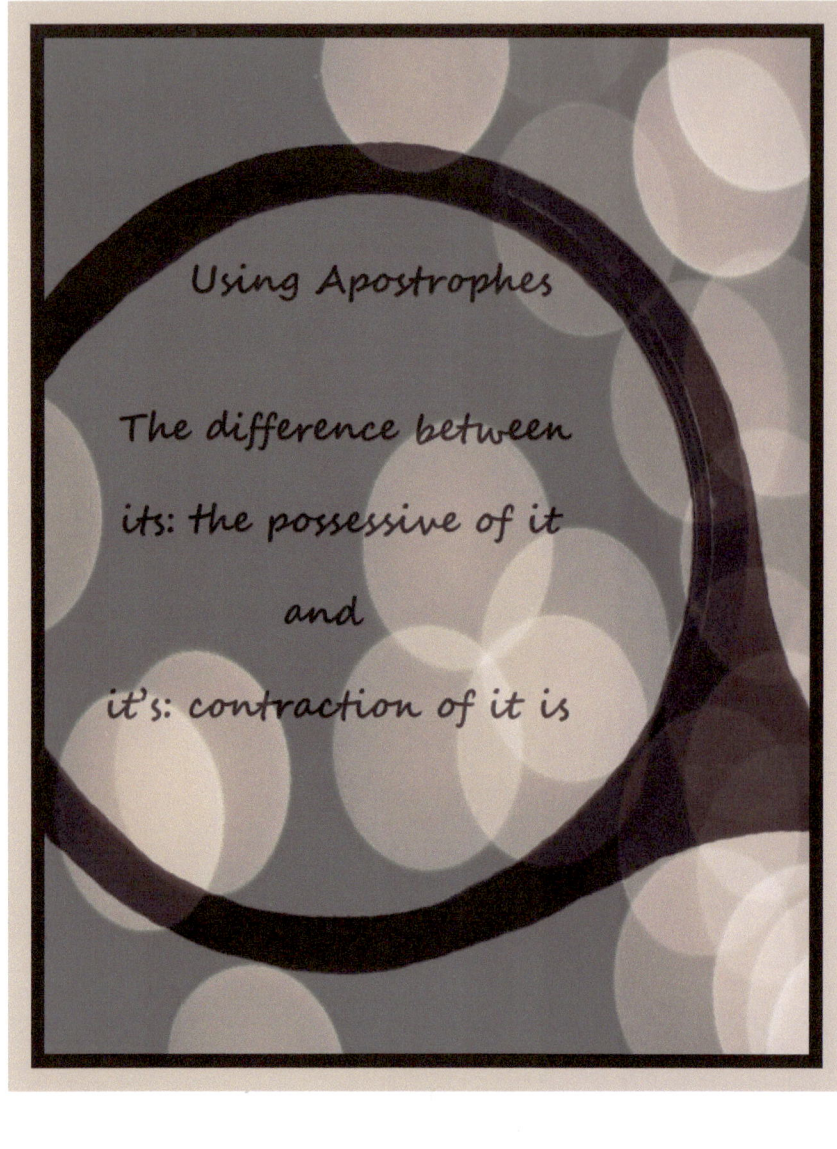

Its/It's

Just simple folk, *his, hers, theirs, its*
reject all accessories,
prance about in the buff.

It's the contraction *it's*
that can't stand silent modesty,
its pet apostrophe
yapping incessantly
that *it's* once was more.

I/Me

I hoards all correctness, misremembered rules
from past classes. Shy of conversation, she stays
clear of chit-chat, casual interludes. Instead,
she insists on her deserved inclusion
in multi-error sentences (direct object or no)
and indignantly sends *Me* scurrying,
comma between his knees. There is no citing
a higher court; no Chicago Style could overturn
her conceited convictions. She, only, has claim
to the brains of beginning brainstormers,
to the doings of final drafts,
to the laws of student editors
systematically deleting *Me*.

Who and Whom

To decide whether to use who or whom, ask a question.

Who wrote Middlemarch?
She wrote it. (Who as subject)

Whom do you trust?
I trust him. (Whom as object)

Whoever, Whomever—Whatever!

is what they say,
what they write
unwittingly of her unfortunate
career. Whomever,
they say (incorrectly), will always be
seen and heard
as object, she with the extra curves
of *m,* the passive stance. We
didn't create the rules; we
empathize, but we
cannot undo the lines of history
penned permanently so many
paragraphs ago.

Try your nose. It's quicker than
   flipping
forty pages of handbook. Anyone
   can tell
an adjective by aroma: flowery,
sweet, a bit like persimmons.

Lean close, sniff deeply,
slowly.

Diagramming Directions

Try your nose. It's quicker than flipping
forty pages of handbook. Anyone can tell
an adjective by aroma: flowery,
sweet, a bit like persimmons.
Nouns knock you out: a blast of smelling salts.
Prepositions tickle the nostrils.
Adverbs vary. Lean close, sniff deeply,
slowly. A potent verb can overpower
any well-meaning descriptor. This
takes talent to tell the two apart. Think
combination for conjunctions: strawberry-banana,
peanut-butter-and-chocolate, mixed-berries.
Articles smell like newsprint,
pronouns like skin, your own. You
have a cold? You can't breathe? Forget it,
call in sick, abracadabra yourself
to tomorrow and try again.

About the Author

Professor of English and Creative Writing at Lock Haven University of Pennsylvania, Sage Graduate Fellow of Cornell University (MFA), and 2023 Monson Arts Fellow, Marjorie Maddox has published fifteen collections of poetry. These include *Transplant, Transport, Transubstantiation* (WordTech, Yellowglen Prize); *Perpendicular As I* (Sandstone Book Award); *Begin with a Question* (Paraclete, International Book Award and Illumination Book Award winner, Catholic Media Book Awards third place recipient); and the ekphrastic collaborations from Shanti Arts *Heart Speaks, Is Spoken For* (with photographer Karen Elias) and *In the Museum of My Daughter's Mind* (with her artist daughter Anna Lee Hafer—www.hafer.work—as well as artists Karen Elias, Greg Mort, Margaret Munz-Losch, Antar Mikosz, Ingo Swann, and Christian Twamley). Forthcoming is *Seeing Things* (Wildhouse 2024).

In addition, Marjorie Maddox has published the story collection *What She Was Saying* (Fomite Press); four children's and YA books—including *Inside Out: Poems on Writing and Reading Poems with Insider Exercises* (Kelsay Books, Finalist International Book Awards), *A Crossing of Zebras: Animal Pacts in Poetry* (Boyd Mills Press/Wipf & Stock), *I'm Feeling Blue, Too!* (Wipf & Stock, a 2021 NCTE Notable Poetry Book), and *Rules of the Game: Baseball Poems* (Boyd Mills Press/Wipf & Stock).

She is assistant editor of *Presence: A Journal of Catholic Poetry* and co-editor, with Jerry Wemple, of two anthologies from Pennsylvania State University Press: *Common Wealth: Contemporary Poets on Pennsylvania* (2005) and *Keystone: Contemporary Poets on Pennsylvania* (2025). She served as host for WPSU's 2023–2024 NPR radio show *Poetry Moment*. The recipient of numerous awards, she gives readings and workshops around the world.

For more information, please see:
www.marjoriemaddox.com

www.ingramcontent.com/pod-product-compliance
Lightning Source LLC
Chambersburg PA
CBHW041426190426
43193CB00036B/16